Handbook of Dairy Technology

MANOJ KUMAR
RAKESH RANJAN
BHARTI SINGH RAIPAT

NOTION PRESS

Handbook of Dairy Technology
First Edition - June, 2025
Pages: 162 (excluding cover)

ISBN: 979-889961992-2
DOI: https://doi.org/10.5281/zenodo.15600906

Department of Zoology,
St. Xavier's College, Ranchi

Printed and published in India
By

Notion Press Media Pvt. Ltd.,
Old No. 38, New No. 6, McNicholas Road, Chetpet, Chennai
Tamil Nadu – 600031
website: www.notionpress.com

मातरः सर्वभूतानां गावः सर्वसुखप्रदाः

Contents

Foreword

The dairy sector plays a vital role in rural livelihoods, food security, and nutritional well-being across India. In the state of **Jharkhand**, where agriculture and livestock are central to the rural economy, the potential for growth and development in the dairy industry is immense. This book, with its comprehensive and practice-oriented approach, serves as a timely and valuable resource for students, extension workers, budding entrepreneurs, and all stakeholders engaged in the dairy value chain.

Beginning with a focused chapter on **"The Dairy Sector in Jharkhand,"** the book explores the unique challenges and opportunities present in the region—highlighting the role of smallholders, indigenous breeds, and cooperative models in shaping the local dairy economy. It goes on to address the foundational principles of **milk quality and adulteration testing**, emphasizing the importance of consumer safety and regulatory compliance.

The chapter on **Clean Milk Production** reinforces the need for hygiene, proper handling, and awareness at the grassroots level—a critical component for ensuring quality at every stage. From there, the book transitions into the technical realm with detailed insights into **milk processing**, followed by **value addition and marketing**, which are essential for enhancing farmer incomes and building sustainable dairy businesses.

Importantly, the book sheds light on **government support mechanisms and entrepreneurship development**, providing readers with a roadmap to access schemes, training, and financial assistance available to the dairy sector. The inclusion of a **practical section**, along with a dedicated chapter on **Dairy Processing Equipment—Principles, Working & Design**, enhances the hands-on learning value of the book.

I commend the authors for their thoughtful structuring and commitment to combining theoretical knowledge with practical application. By contextualizing dairy technology within Jharkhand's socio-economic landscape, this book bridges the gap between academic knowledge and real-world needs. It is an indispensable guide for anyone looking to understand or contribute to the modernization and sustainability of dairy farming in India.

I sincerely hope that this book will inspire a new generation of dairy professionals, entrepreneurs, and change-makers committed to quality, innovation, and inclusive growth.

Dr. Father Robert Pradeep Kujur, S.J.

Principal
St. Xavier's College,
Ranchi

Preface

The science and technology of milk and dairy products have evolved tremendously over the past century, transforming the way we produce, process, preserve, and consume one of the most important food groups in human nutrition. This book on **Dairy Technology** is an effort to present a comprehensive and practical account of the principles, practices, and innovations that define the modern dairy industry.

From traditional methods of milk handling to the latest advancements in processing, quality control, and product development, this book is intended to serve as a foundational resource for students, professionals, researchers, and practitioners in the dairy and food industries. It covers a wide spectrum of topics—ranging from milk composition and microbial safety to emerging technologies in dairy product formulation and automation in processing lines.

The need for this book arises from a growing demand for technically sound and accessible information on dairy science and technology. Whether it's understanding the biochemistry of milk, mastering pasteurization protocols, or navigating regulatory standards, the reader will find concise explanations supported by real-world examples and illustrations.

This work is the result of collaborative efforts, academic insights, and industrial experience. We have attempted to strike a balance between theory and application, ensuring that the content is both informative and practically relevant.

We would like to express sincere gratitude to all contributors, colleagues, industry experts, and students whose feedback and encouragement shaped the development of this text. Special thanks go to the educators and professionals who continue to inspire progress and innovation in the field of dairy technology.

It is our hope that this book will contribute meaningfully to the learning and advancement of readers, and foster a deeper appreciation of the science behind every drop of milk and every dairy product on the shelf.

-Authors

Acknowledgments

The journey of bringing this book on Dairy Technology to fruition has been both enriching and enlightening. We are grateful to all those who contributed to its development.

We would also like to acknowledge the contributions of the research scientists, industry experts, and dairy technologists whose work provided valuable insights and data that informed the content of this book.

To our colleagues and peers, thank you for your critical feedback, encouragement, and for engaging in thoughtful discussions that helped shape the direction of this work.

We are also indebted to the editorial and publishing team for their professional support and for guiding this book through each stage of its development.

This book is dedicated to all those committed to the advancement of dairy science and to the improvement of dairy practices worldwide.

- Authors

Introduction

Dairy farming holds a deep-rooted place in the agricultural history of the world, and especially in India, where it has been practiced for thousands of years. Traditionally, dairy farming was a community-driven activity, centred around indigenous cattle breeds and age-old methods of milking and milk preservation. Over time, with the advent of science and innovation, the sector has witnessed a remarkable transformation.

Modern dairy technology has revolutionized the way milk is produced, processed, and distributed. From automated milking machines to advanced cold chain systems and quality testing tools, these technological advancements have significantly enhanced efficiency, hygiene, and productivity. This progress not only ensures better returns for farmers but also delivers high-quality milk and dairy products to consumers.

In Indian culture, milk is more than just a source of nutrition—it is a symbol of purity and an essential part of daily rituals, religious offerings, and traditional cuisine. From sacred practices involving milk offerings to its role in festivals like Janmashtami and Pongal, dairy has spiritual and cultural importance across the country.

The growing relevance of dairy technology is pivotal not only for improving milk yield and quality but also for ensuring food security, boosting rural development, and addressing environmental challenges. It opens doors to innovation in value-added products, packaging, and sustainability practices.

Moreover, dairy farming and allied industries have emerged as a powerful means of self-employment, especially in rural India. With relatively low initial investment and consistent demand for dairy products, it offers a viable livelihood option for millions. Empowering farmers, especially women and smallholders, through training and technology can lead to inclusive economic growth and rural empowerment.

In this context, the fusion of tradition with technology holds the key to building a sustainable, productive, and culturally rich dairy sector in India.

1. The Dairy Sector in Jharkhand

1. Status of Milk Production and Consumption in Jharkhand

Jharkhand has made significant strides in milk production over the past decade, largely due to the collaboration with the National Dairy Development Board (NDDB) since 2014.

- **Increased Production:** The state's annual milk production capacity nearly doubled from 17.34 lakh tonnes in 2014-15 to **30.25 lakh tonnes in 2023-24**.

- **Per Capita Availability:** The per capita availability of milk has also increased substantially from 137 grams per day in 2014-15 to **209 grams per day in 2024**. This still lags behind the national average, which stood at **471 grams per day in 2023-24**.

- **Daily Production:** The total daily milk production in Jharkhand is around **70 lakh litres**.

- **Surplus Availability:** Approximately **35 lakh litres** are surplus after domestic consumption and are available for the organized packaged milk sector.

- **Key Players:** The Jharkhand Milk Federation (JMF), operating under the brand name **Medha**, is a major player, currently procuring about **3.75 lakh litres** of milk per day from farmers. Other significant brands in the urban sector include Sudha and Amul.

- **Future Targets:** JMF aims to procure and produce **5 lakh litres of milk per day by 2029**.

- **Infrastructure Development:** JMF is working on establishing new dairy plants in Jamshedpur and Giridih, each with a 50,000 to 1 lakh litre daily capacity. Additionally, a power plant and a dairy product plant are proposed in Ranchi to further boost the sector.

- **Farmer Engagement:** The number of farmers involved in dairy activities has increased significantly from a few thousand to over one lakh in the last decade, supported by training programs on animal husbandry.

- **Government Support:** The dairy sector is a thrust area for the Jharkhand government, with various incentive schemes to promote dairy activities. The incentive for milk producers affiliated with JMF was recently increased to **₹5 per litre**.

Current Status of Milk Consumption:

Despite the increase in production, Jharkhand still faces a gap between milk production and consumption.

- **Urban Demand:** The total demand in urban sectors is around **14 lakh litres per day**, out of which about **7 lakh litres** are met by packaged milk.

- **Organized Sector Supply:** Medha produces around 2 to 2.5 lakh litres daily, Sudha about 3 lakh litres, and Amul approximately 1.75 lakh litres, with smaller players contributing the rest.

- **Consumption Pattern:** There is reportedly a lower awareness about milk consumption among the tribal population in the state.

- **Deficit:** Jharkhand still relies on milk procured from neighboring states like Bihar and West Bengal to meet its demand.

- **Per Capita Consumption vs. National Average:** The per capita milk consumption in Jharkhand is significantly lower than the national average. In 2024, the per capita availability was 209 grams per day, compared to the national average of 471 grams per day. The state government aims to increase this to 237 grams per day in 2024-25.

Detailed Review:

- **Positive Trends:** Jharkhand has demonstrated strong growth in milk production, indicating the success of initiatives like the collaboration with NDDB and the establishment of JMF. The increased per capita availability reflects improved access to milk for the population. The government's focus and financial incentives are likely to further boost the dairy sector.
- **Challenges:** The state still grapples with a considerable demand-supply gap, particularly in urban areas. The lower per capita consumption compared to the national average suggests a need to promote milk consumption across all sections of the population. Dependence on neighboring states for milk supply highlights the need for continued efforts to achieve self-sufficiency.

- **Opportunities:** There is significant potential for further development of the dairy sector in Jharkhand, given the increasing livestock population and the demand for milk and milk products. Expanding the infrastructure for milk processing and procurement, as planned by JMF, will be crucial. Raising awareness about the benefits of milk consumption, especially in rural and tribal areas, can also drive demand. Dairy farming offers a significant opportunity for income generation and employment, especially for small and marginal farmers.

In conclusion, while Jharkhand has made commendable progress in milk production, there is still a considerable way to go to achieve self-sufficiency and match the national average in per capita milk consumption. Continued focus on infrastructure development, farmer support, and promoting consumption will be key to realizing the full potential of the dairy sector in the state.

2. Indigenous Cattle and Dairy Cooperatives

Indigenous Cattle Breeds

While Jharkhand boasts a significant population of indigenous cattle, it's noteworthy that as of May 20, 2025, **no specific cattle breed from Jharkhand has been officially recognized and registered at the national level.** The majority of the indigenous cattle in the state are categorized as **non-descript**, meaning they haven't been formally characterized and documented as distinct breeds.

However, research has identified a unique cattle population within Jharkhand, often referred to as **Jharkhandi cattle** or sometimes locally as **Medini cattle**, which shows potential for recognition as the state's first indigenous breed.

Figure 1: Medini breed - Jharkhand

Characteristics of Indigenous Cattle in Jharkhand (Primarily based on observations of the non-descript population and the prospective Jharkhandi/Medini breed):

- **Adaptation to Local Conditions:** These cattle have evolved over generations to thrive in the specific agro-climatic conditions of Jharkhand, including its variable terrain, heat, humidity, and prevalent diseases. They exhibit good tolerance to these local stressors.

- **Low Input-Low Output System:** They are typically managed under traditional, low-input systems with minimal external resources. Their productivity reflects this management style.
- **Morphological Traits:** Research on the Jharkhandi cattle has highlighted some characteristic physical features, including:
    - **Pre-scapular hump:** The hump is located over the shoulders, a typical feature of *Bos indicus* cattle.
    - **Moderate size:** They are generally medium-sized animals.
    - Other morphometric measurements have been recorded in research studies, providing a baseline for future breed characterization.
- **Genetic Diversity:** Genetic analysis using microsatellite markers has revealed substantial genetic variation within the Jharkhandi cattle population. This genetic diversity is a valuable resource for adaptation and breeding.
- **Disease Resistance:** Like many indigenous breeds, they are generally considered to have better resistance to local diseases compared to exotic breeds.
- **Draught Power:** While specific data on draught capabilities in Jharkhand is limited for categorized breeds, non-descript indigenous

cattle often play a role in agricultural tasks for small and marginal farmers.

- **Milk Production:** Milk yield in non-descript indigenous cattle in Jharkhand is generally low, with averages reported around 1.5 kg per cow per day. However, the Jharkhandi/Medini cattle show potential for higher milk production compared to the general non-descript population.
- **Economic Importance:** Indigenous cattle are crucial for the rural economy of Jharkhand, particularly for tribal communities and smallholder farmers. They provide:
    - **Milk:** A source of nutrition and income.
    - **Manure:** Used as organic fertilizer, contributing to soil health.
    - **Draught power:** For ploughing, transportation, and other agricultural activities (though this is decreasing with mechanization).
    - **Livelihood security:** Livestock rearing, including cattle, often supplements income from agriculture and other sources, especially in regions with rain-fed agriculture.
    - **Social and cultural significance:** Livestock often holds cultural value within tribal communities.

3. Efforts Towards Breed Recognition and Conservation:

- **Research and Characterization:** Studies, such as the one published in *Animal Biotechnology* in 2022, have focused on the morphometric and genetic characterization of Jharkhandi cattle. These efforts aim to establish their distinct genetic identity and provide the scientific basis for breed registration.
- **Government Initiatives:** The Jharkhand government recognizes the importance of livestock and has implemented policies aimed at genetic upgradation of local cattle. While the focus has often been on crossbreeding with recognized Indian breeds like Sahiwal, Red Sindhi, and Gir to improve milk production, there is a growing need to conserve and develop the unique indigenous genetic resources of the state.
- **Jharkhand Gau Sewa Ayog:** This state-level commission works for the welfare and protection of cattle in Jharkhand. Its objectives include promoting the preservation of germplasm of indigenous/local cattle breeds.
- **Rashtriya Gokul Mission:** This national program aims to conserve and develop indigenous bovine breeds. While specific projects in Jharkhand focusing solely on the state's unique indigenous cattle aren't explicitly detailed in readily available information, the state likely

benefits from the mission's broader objectives, including establishing IVF labs for indigenous breed development.

- **Need for Formal Registration:** The research community emphasizes the importance of formally registering the Jharkhandi (Medini) cattle as an official breed. This would pave the way for scientific management, sustainable utilization, and focused conservation efforts to prevent genetic dilution.

Challenges and Way Forward:

- **Genetic Dilution:** Crossbreeding with non-native breeds poses a threat to the unique genetic makeup of indigenous cattle populations in Jharkhand.
- **Lack of Documentation:** The "non-descript" categorization highlights the need for comprehensive phenotypic and genetic characterization of local cattle.

- **Awareness and Promotion:** Raising awareness among local communities about the value and importance of conserving indigenous breeds is crucial.
- **Structured Breeding Programs:** Implementing well-designed breeding programs can help improve the productivity of indigenous cattle

while maintaining their adaptability and resilience.

In conclusion, while Jharkhand is home to a significant number of indigenous cattle that play a vital role in the local economy and livelihoods, no breed from the state has yet achieved official national recognition. However, ongoing research on the distinct Jharkhandi (Medini) cattle population offers a promising path towards recognizing and conserving this valuable genetic resource for the benefit of the state's agricultural and tribal communities. Continued efforts in research, characterization, and focused conservation initiatives are essential to safeguard Jharkhand's unique bovine biodiversity.

Indigenous cattle of India

India is blessed with a rich diversity of indigenous cattle breeds, well-adapted to the country's varied agro-climatic conditions. These breeds have evolved over centuries to be resilient to local diseases, perform on low-quality feed, and tolerate heat stress. They are categorized based on their primary utility:

Milch Breeds (High Milk Production):

- **Sahiwal:** Originating from the Montgomery district of undivided India (now in Pakistan), it's considered the best indigenous dairy breed, known for high milk yield, heat tolerance, and disease resistance.

Figure 2: Sahiwal

Figure 3: Red Sindhi

- **Red Sindhi:** Native to the Karachi and Hyderabad regions of Pakistan, it's known for its high milk production and adaptability to hot climates.

Figure 4: Gir

Figure 5: Tharparkar

Figure 6: Rathi

Figure 7: Deoni

- **Gir:** Found in the Gir forests of Gujarat, it's known for its high milk yield, disease resistance, and distinctive appearance with a bulging forehead and long, pendulous ears.

- **Tharparkar:** Originating from the Tharparkar district of Pakistan and found in Rajasthan and Gujarat, it's a dual-purpose breed known for both milk production and draught power, as well as its adaptability to arid conditions.
- **Rathi:** Found in Rajasthan, it's a good milch breed.
- **Deoni:** Originating from Maharashtra and Karnataka, it's a dual-purpose breed with moderate milk production.

Draught Breeds (Strong for Work):

- **Hallikar:** From Karnataka, known for its strength, endurance, and trotting ability, making it excellent for agricultural work and transportation.

Figure 8: Hallikar

- **Amritmahal:** Originating in Karnataka, developed for draught purposes, known for their endurance and speed.
- **Khillari:** From Maharashtra and Karnataka, resembles Hallikar, known for its fast and powerful bullocks.

Figure 9: Amritmahal

Figure 10: Khillari

Figure 11: Kangayam

- **Kangayam:** Native to Tamil Nadu, known for its strength and suitability for agricultural operations.
- **Bargur:** Found in the hilly regions of Tamil Nadu, adapted for work in uneven terrain, known for speed and endurance.

Figure 12: Bargur

Figure 13: Umblachery

Figure 14: Nagori

- **Umblachery:** From Tamil Nadu, well-suited for wet ploughing and known for its sturdiness.
- **Nagori:** From Rajasthan, appreciated for its fast road work.
- **Malvi:** From Madhya Pradesh, a powerful draught breed.

- **Kenkatha (Kenwariya):** From Uttar Pradesh and Madhya Pradesh, primarily a draught breed.
- **Kherigarh:** From Uttar Pradesh, known for its draught capabilities.
- **Ponwar:** From Uttar Pradesh, used for draught purposes.
- **Siri:** Found in Sikkim and West Bengal, primarily used for draught.
- **Bachaur:** From Bihar, mainly used for draught.
- **Ghumusari:** From Odisha, a draught breed.
- **Khariar:** From Odisha, used for draught.
- **Kosali:** From Chhattisgarh, a draught breed.
- **Belahi:** From Haryana and Chandigarh, used for milk and draught.
- **Gangatiri:** From Uttar Pradesh and Bihar, a dual-purpose breed.
- **Badri:** From Uttarakhand, used for milk and draught.
- **Ladakhi:** From Jammu and Kashmir, used for draught.
- **Thutho:** From Nagaland, used for draught and meat.
- **Konkan Kapila:** From Maharashtra and Goa, a draught breed.

Figure 15: Malvi

Figure 16: Kenkatha

Figure 17: Kherigarh

Figure 18: Ponwar

Figure 19: Siri

Figure 20: Bachaur

Figure 21: Ghumusari

Figure 22: Khariar

Figure 23: Kosali

Figure 24: Belahi

Figure 25: Gangatiri

Figure 26: Badri

Figure 27: Ladakhi

Figure 28: Thutho

Figure 29: Konkan Kapila

Dual-Purpose Breeds (Good for both Milk and Draught):

- **Hariana:** From Haryana, known for its powerful bullocks and fair milk-producing cows.
- **Kankrej:** Originating from Gujarat and Rajasthan, the heaviest Indian breed, known for fast and powerful draught capabilities and good milk production.
- **Ongole:** From Andhra Pradesh, known for its strength, disease resistance, and adaptability to tropical climates, used for both agriculture and milk.
- **Krishna Valley:** From the border region of Maharashtra and Andhra Pradesh, large animals used for slow ploughing and valued for their working qualities, with moderate milk production.

Figure 30: Some Dual-Purpose Breeds of Cow

- **Gaolao:** From Maharashtra and Madhya Pradesh, used for milk and draught.
- **Mewati (Kosi):** From Haryana and Rajasthan, primarily a draught breed with some milking ability.

- **Nimari:** From Madhya Pradesh and Maharashtra.
- **Poda Thurpu:** From Telangana, a draught purpose breed.
- **Nari:** From Rajasthan and Gujarat, a dual-purpose breed.
- **Binjharpuri:** From Odisha, used for milk and draught.
- **Lakhimi:** From Assam, used for milk and draught.

Other Notable Breeds:

- **Vechur:** From Kerala, one of the smallest cattle breeds globally, known for high-fat content milk and medicinal properties. It is critically endangered.
- **Punganur:** From Andhra Pradesh, a dwarf breed known for its low feed intake and milk with high fat content.
- **Kasaragod:** From Kerala.
- **Malenadu Gidda:** From the coastal and hilly areas of Karnataka.
- **Motu:** From Odisha, Chhattisgarh, and Andhra Pradesh.
- **Gangatiri:** From Uttar Pradesh and Bihar.
- **Shweta Kapila:** From Goa.
- **Himachali Pahari:** From Himachal Pradesh.
- **Dagri:** From Gujarat, a draught breed.

- **Red Kandhari:** From Maharashtra.

Characteristics of Indigenous Cattle:

- **Adaptability:** Well-suited to the local climate, including heat and humidity.
- **Disease Resistance:** Generally, possess better resistance to tropical diseases and parasites compared to exotic breeds.
- **Low Input Requirement:** Can survive and produce on poor quality feed and fodder.
- **Heat Tolerance:** Have physiological mechanisms for efficient heat dissipation, such as more sweat glands and loose skin.
- **Hardiness:** Known for their ability to withstand stressful environmental conditions.
- **Genetic Diversity:** Represent a valuable reservoir of genetic diversity.

Conservation Efforts:

The Indian government and various organizations are undertaking efforts to conserve and promote indigenous cattle breeds through schemes like the **Rashtriya Gokul Mission**, which aims to:

- Establish **Gokul Grams** (integrated indigenous cattle centres).
- Strengthen **bull mother farms** to conserve high genetic merit animals.

- Implement **field performance recording** to identify elite animals.
- Support the establishment of **breeders' societies**.
- Promote the use of **disease-free, high genetic merit bulls** for natural service.
- Provide **incentives to farmers** maintaining elite indigenous animals.
- Utilize advanced reproductive technologies like **artificial insemination (AI)** and **in-vitro fertilization (IVF)**.
- Conduct **genomic studies** for breed improvement.

These efforts are crucial for preserving the unique genetic heritage of India's indigenous cattle and ensuring their continued contribution to the agricultural economy and rural livelihoods.

4. Dairy Cooperatives

Dairy cooperatives play a crucial role in the milk production and distribution landscape of Jharkhand. Here's a detailed overview:

Key Players:

- **Jharkhand State Cooperative Milk Producers' Federation Ltd. (JMF):** This is the apex body for dairy cooperatives in the state, operating under the brand name **Medha**. Established in

June 2013 and operationalized in August 2014 with the support of the National Dairy Development Board (NDDB), JMF aims to promote dairying as a livelihood source and make Jharkhand self-sufficient in milk production.

- **Functions:** JMF is involved in milk procurement from village-level milk producer groups, processing, and marketing of milk and milk products across Jharkhand.
- **Reach:** As of May 2025, JMF procures milk from over one lakh farmers across 15 districts of Jharkhand.
- **Infrastructure:** JMF operates dairy processing plants in Ranchi (Hotwar), Deoghar, Koderma, and Latehar, with a total installed capacity of 140 thousand litres per day (TLPD). A new 1 lakh litre capacity plant was established in Ranchi with NDDB's support. There's also a cattle feed plant in Ranchi.
- **Future Expansion:** JMF is working on establishing new dairy plants in Jamshedpur and Giridih (each with 50,000 to 1 lakh litre daily capacity) and a dairy product plant in Ranchi to further increase processing capacity to 5 lakh litres per day by 2024 (likely achieved or nearing).

- **Farmer Support:** JMF provides various support services to milk producers, including quality cattle feed at subsidized rates, veterinary helplines ("Gaupalak Sahayata Kendra"), productivity enhancement camps, and training programs. Payments for milk supplied by farmers are directly deposited into their bank accounts every 10 days.
- **Milk Collection:** JMF is establishing village-based computerized milk collection systems with bulk milk coolers to ensure quality and efficient procurement.
- **Products:** Medha offers a range of milk products, including standard milk, toned milk, tea special milk, paneer, dahi, misti dahi, misti lassi, salted lassi, peda, and ghee.

- **Primary Village-Level Cooperative Societies:** These are the base-level organizations where individual milk producers become members. They are responsible for:
  - Collecting milk from their members.
  - Conducting initial quality testing and weighing.
  - Facilitating the transportation of milk to JMF's processing centres.

  - Disbursing payments to their members based on the quantity and quality of milk supplied.
  - Acting as a link between the farmers and the federation for various support services and training.

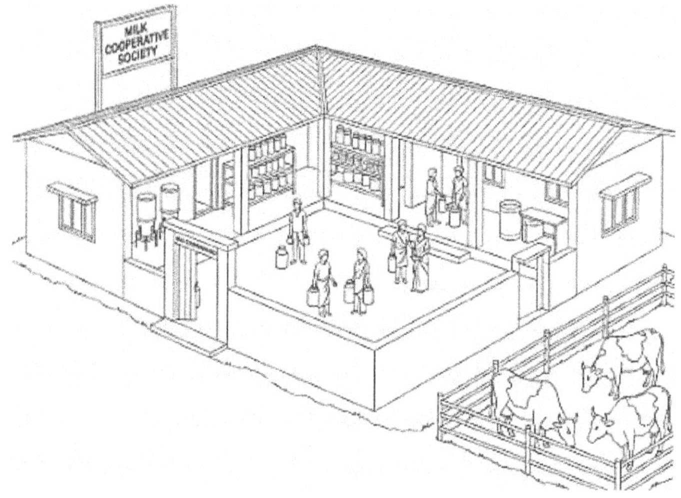

Figure 31: Diagrammatic representation of a Milk Co-operative society

- **District-Level Cooperative Unions:** These may exist to coordinate the activities of the primary societies within a district and facilitate better linkages with the state federation. Information on the specific structure and prevalence of district-level unions in Jharkhand is less readily available, suggesting the primary focus is on the strong link between village societies and JMF.

Impact and Significance:

- **Livelihood Improvement:** Dairy cooperatives, particularly through JMF's initiatives, have significantly contributed to improving the socio-economic status of dairy farmers in Jharkhand by providing a stable market for their milk and regular income.
- **Increased Milk Production:** The organized structure of cooperatives and the support provided to farmers have played a key role in the substantial increase in milk production in Jharkhand over the past decade.
- **Empowerment of Rural Communities:** Dairy cooperatives empower rural communities, including tribal populations, by offering alternative employment opportunities beyond traditional agriculture and mining.
- **Quality Assurance:** The cooperative structure emphasizes quality testing at the village level and ensures that consumers receive hygienic and unadulterated milk and milk products under the Medha brand.
- **Financial Inclusion:** Direct bank transfers for milk payments promote financial inclusion among rural farmers.

Challenges:

- **Demand-Supply Gap:** Despite the progress, Jharkhand still faces a gap between milk production and consumption, relying on neighboring states to meet the demand.

Cooperatives need to continue scaling up production.

- **Awareness and Consumption:** There's a need to further promote milk consumption, especially in rural and tribal areas, to increase local demand.
- **Infrastructure Development:** While JMF has expanded its infrastructure, continuous investment in processing plants, chilling centers, and transportation networks is crucial to handle increasing milk volumes.
- **Genetic Improvement:** Further efforts are needed to improve the productivity of local cattle through better breeding practices and access to quality semen.
- **Financial Sustainability of Primary Societies:** Ensuring the financial viability and efficient management of the primary village-level cooperatives is essential for the long-term success of the dairy sector.

In conclusion, dairy cooperatives, with the Jharkhand State Cooperative Milk Producers' Federation (Medha) at the forefront, form a vital part of the state's dairy sector. They have played a significant role in increasing milk production, improving farmers' livelihoods, and providing quality milk to consumers. Continued focus on strengthening the cooperative structure, expanding infrastructure, and addressing the existing challenges will be crucial for achieving self-sufficiency in milk production and further empowering the rural communities of Jharkhand.

5. Dairy Brands in Jharkhand

Based on the information available, here are some of the major and other dairy brands with a presence in Jharkhand as of May 20, 2025:

Major Dairy Brands:

- **Medha Dairy:** This is the flagship brand of the **Jharkhand State Cooperative Milk Producers' Federation Ltd. (JMF)**. It is the most significant local player, with a wide reach and product portfolio, focusing on empowering Jharkhand's dairy farmers.
- **Sudha Dairy:** While primarily based in Bihar, **Bihar State Milk Co-operative Federation Ltd. (COMFED)'s** brand, Sudha, has a substantial presence in Jharkhand, with processing units and a wide distribution network across many districts.
- **Amul:** This is a major national dairy cooperative brand from Gujarat that has a significant market share in Jharkhand's urban areas.
- **Osam Dairy:** This appears to be a private sector dairy brand with operations in Eastern India, including Jharkhand. They are known for some innovative products like flavored yogurts.

Other Dairy Brands and Suppliers in Jharkhand (primarily in Ranchi):

- **Puresh Daily:** A local brand in Ranchi offering online ordering.
- **Shatakshi Agrotech:** Based in Ranchi.
- **Farm Dairy:** Located in Ranchi.
- **Milky Kool:** A Ranchi-based dairy.
- **R S Foods:** Operating in Ranchi.
- **Shubh Sri Dairy:** Based in Ranchi.
- **Jharkhand Dairy Pvt Ltd:** Located in Ranchi.
- **R Star Organic Research and Training Dairy:** Based in Ranchi.
- **Ranchi Dairy:** A local dairy in Ranchi.
- **ITC Aashirvaad Svasti:** A national conglomerate that entered the Jharkhand dairy market in September 2023 with milk, curd, paneer, lassi, and mishti doi.
- **The A2 Dairy:** Based in Ranchi, focusing on A2 milk products.
- **Military Dairy Farm:** Located in Ranchi.
- **Krishna Dairy:** Based in Namkum, Ranchi.
- **Berry Dairy:** Located in Ranchi.
- **MOLU Pure Cow Milk Product:** Serves Ranchi.

Important Considerations:

- **Market Share:** While Medha, Sudha, and Amul are likely the largest players in terms of volume, the market share of each can fluctuate.
- **Regional Presence:** Some of the smaller brands might have a stronger presence in specific localities within Jharkhand.
- **Product Focus:** Some brands might specialize in certain types of dairy products (e.g., A2 milk by The A2 Dairy).
- **Availability:** The availability of these brands can vary across different parts of Jharkhand (urban vs. rural).

This list provides a good overview of the prominent dairy brands you'll find in Jharkhand as of today. Medha and Sudha, being cooperatives with a strong focus on local procurement, play a particularly important role in the state's dairy economy.

6. Scope for Rural Dairy Entrepreneurship

The dairy sector in Jharkhand presents significant opportunities for rural entrepreneurship. Small-scale family farms dominate the industry, accounting for approximately 80% of milk production. These farms typically maintain small herds and produce milk primarily for household consumption. However, with the growing demand for milk and milk products, there is potential for these small-scale operations to expand and commercialize.

The state government supports dairy entrepreneurship through various initiatives, including subsidies for milch cow distribution to Below Poverty Line (BPL) women, technical input programs, breed improvement schemes, and training and extension services. Furthermore, the establishment of infrastructure such as milk processing plants and cattle feed plants enhances the viability of dairy enterprises.

The growing urban demand for milk, coupled with the state's efforts to improve dairy infrastructure and support services, creates a conducive environment for rural entrepreneurs to invest in dairy farming. By leveraging government schemes and cooperative structures, rural entrepreneurs can contribute to the state's goal of achieving self-reliance in milk production while improving their livelihoods.

Conclusion

Jharkhand's dairy sector has made commendable progress in recent years, with increased milk production, the establishment of dairy cooperatives, and initiatives to improve indigenous cattle breeds. However, challenges remain in bridging the demand-supply gap and enhancing per capita milk availability. By continuing to support rural dairy entrepreneurship and strengthening cooperative structures, Jharkhand can move towards self-sufficiency in milk production and improved livelihoods for its rural population.

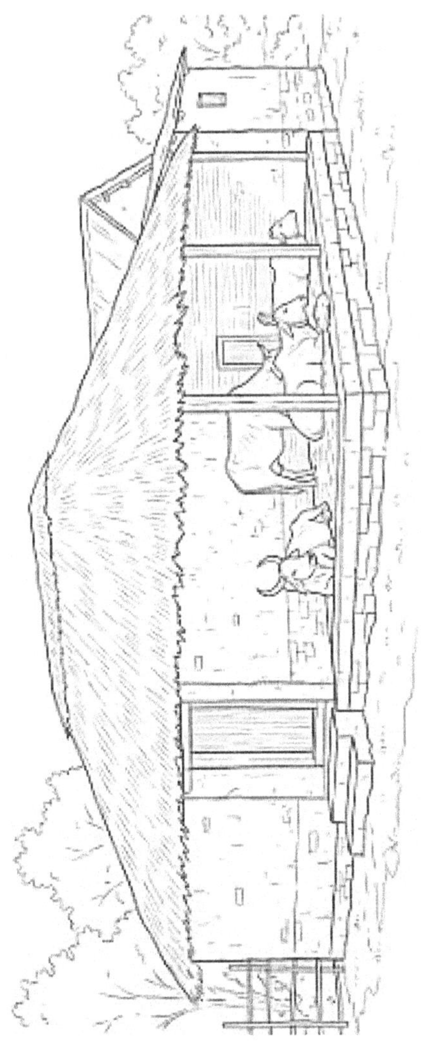

2. Milk Quality & Adulteration tests

Milk is one of the most complete natural foods, widely consumed across the globe due to its nutritional value. However, ensuring its quality is crucial for safeguarding public health and maintaining consumer trust. This chapter covers the essential components of milk composition, common tests used to assess milk quality, and simple techniques to detect adulteration.

Figure 32: A boy testing milk quality at home

1. Milk Composition: Fat, SNF, and Water

Milk is a complex emulsion consisting of various nutrients essential for human growth and development. The three main components that determine its quality are **Fat**, **Solids-Not-Fat (SNF)**, and **Water**.

1.1 Fat

Milk fat is the most valuable component from a commercial point of view. It provides energy, essential fatty acids, and fat-soluble vitamins like A, D, E, and K.

- **Standard fat percentage in cow milk**: ~3.5% to 4.5%
- **Standard fat percentage in buffalo milk**: ~6.5% to 7.5%

1.2 Solids-Not-Fat (SNF)

SNF includes proteins (casein and whey), lactose (milk sugar), and minerals (calcium, phosphorus, etc.).

- **Standard SNF content in cow milk**: ~8% to 9%
- **Standard SNF content in buffalo milk**: ~9% to 10%

1.3 Water

Water is the major constituent, making up about 83% to 87% of the total milk volume. Any excessive dilution beyond natural levels is considered adulteration.

---

2. Tests for Milk Quality

To ensure that milk meets quality standards, several tests are employed. These can be categorized into **physical**, **chemical**, and **sensory (organoleptic)** assessments.

2.1 Use of Lactometer

A **lactometer** is an instrument used to determine the density (specific gravity) of milk.

- **Principle**: Pure milk has a density of approximately 1.028 to 1.032 g/cm^3.
- **How it works**: The lactometer floats in a milk sample, and the reading is taken at the milk surface level. A low reading may indicate water adulteration.
- **Limitations**: It cannot detect other types of adulterants or distinguish between naturally low-density milk and watered milk.

2.2 Alcohol Test

This test helps determine the **stability of milk proteins**, especially before heat processing.

- **Procedure**: Equal volumes of milk and ethanol (usually 75%) are mixed.
- **Observation**: If milk curdles, it indicates poor protein stability, often due to high acidity or mastitis-affected milk.
- **Significance**: Helps identify milk that may spoil during pasteurization.

2.3 Organoleptic Testing

Organoleptic testing involves the use of **human senses** to assess milk quality:

- **Appearance**: Pure milk should be clean, free from foreign particles, and have a white or creamy color.
- **Smell**: Fresh milk has a mild, pleasant aroma. A sour or foul smell indicates spoilage.
- **Taste**: Slightly sweet and creamy. Any bitterness or unusual taste suggests contamination or spoilage.
- **Texture**: Smooth and fluid; any sliminess or clumps suggest microbial growth.

---

3. Simple Adulteration Detection Techniques

Adulteration of milk is a widespread issue, especially in regions lacking strict quality controls. Below are some **common adulterants** and **simple household techniques** to detect them:

Adulterant	**Purpose**	**Detection Method**
Water	To increase volume	Use lactometer; abnormal drop in reading (<1.026) indicates dilution

Adulterant	Purpose	Detection Method
Starch	To mimic SNF	Add a few drops of iodine solution to milk. Blue coloration confirms presence
Detergent	For artificial froth	Shake milk. Persistent foamy layer and soapy feel suggest detergent
Urea	To increase SNF and shelf life	Mix with p-DMAC reagent (in labs) or sniff for pungent ammonia odor
Formalin	To increase shelf life	Add sulfuric acid along the test tube sides. Purple ring confirms adulteration
Synthetic Milk	Made with soap, urea, etc.	Bitter taste, yellowish tinge, and froth formation on shaking
Salt	To mask dilution	Conduct silver nitrate test or taste directly (salty milk is unnatural)
Sugar	To mimic lactose	Benedict's solution test (requires lab setup)

Tips for Consumers:

- Boiling milk does not remove chemical adulterants.

- Always source milk from trusted vendors or certified cooperatives.
- Use testing kits provided by food safety authorities for home checks.

Conclusion

Milk quality assurance is essential to maintain nutritional standards and prevent health hazards. Understanding milk composition and being familiar with basic quality and adulteration tests empowers producers and consumers alike. With simple tools like lactometers and household detection methods, one can identify impure milk and take informed action. Combined efforts from producers, regulators, and consumers are crucial to ensuring that milk, often termed "liquid white gold," remains pure and beneficial for all.

3. Clean Milk Production

Clean milk production is the cornerstone of a healthy and sustainable dairy industry. It not only ensures the safety and quality of milk for consumers but also improves the shelf life and market value of milk. Clean milk refers to milk that is free from dirt, pathogenic microorganisms, residues of harmful chemicals, and other contaminants. This chapter explores the importance of hygiene in milking and transport, emphasizes personal and equipment hygiene, and describes simple cooling and preservation techniques suitable for rural and small-scale dairy settings.

---

1. Importance of Hygiene in Milking and Transport

1.1 Hygiene During Milking

Milk is highly susceptible to contamination due to its rich nutrient content and warm temperature when freshly drawn. Most microbial contamination occurs at the time of milking due to unhygienic conditions.

Benefits of hygienic milking:

- Improves milk safety by reducing bacterial load.
- Minimizes spoilage and increases shelf life.

- Prevents transmission of zoonotic diseases (e.g., brucellosis, tuberculosis).
- Enhances acceptability and value in formal markets.

Sources of contamination during milking:

- Dirty udders and teats.
- Contaminated hands of the milkers.
- Use of unclean utensils and equipment.
- Dust, flies, and animal waste in the milking area.

Best practices:

- Wash the udder and teats with clean lukewarm water and dry with a clean cloth before milking.
- Discard the first few streams of milk (foremilk), which may contain a high microbial load.
- Use individual clean towels for each animal to avoid cross-contamination.
- Milk in a calm, dust-free environment—preferably in a covered or shaded area.

1.2 Hygiene During Milk Transport

Once milk is collected, its cleanliness must be maintained during transport to chilling centers or markets.

Key precautions:

- Use stainless steel or food-grade plastic containers. Avoid containers made of iron, aluminum, or non-food-grade plastics.

- Transport milk in covered containers to prevent entry of dust and insects.
- Do not mix morning and evening milk without cooling.
- Avoid long delays between milking and chilling; bacteria multiply rapidly at ambient temperatures.

Impact of poor hygiene in transport:

- Rapid spoilage due to microbial growth.
- Risk of chemical contamination.
- Loss of fat and SNF due to oxidation or enzyme activity.

---

2. Personal and Equipment Hygiene

2.1 Personal Hygiene of the Milker

The individual performing the milking plays a critical role in ensuring milk hygiene. Poor personal hygiene can result in contamination with bacteria from the skin, wounds, or respiratory tract.

Recommended practices:

- Wash hands with soap and clean water before and after milking.
- Keep fingernails trimmed and avoid wearing jewellery.

- Wear clean clothing or an apron specifically for milking.
- Cover any open wounds on the hands with clean, waterproof bandages.
- Avoid smoking, spitting, or eating during milking.

2.2 Equipment Hygiene

Milking utensils and containers are common sources of contamination if not cleaned properly.

Ideal equipment cleaning steps:

1. **Rinse** the utensils with lukewarm water immediately after use to remove milk residues.
2. **Scrub** with hot water and detergent to eliminate fat and protein films.
3. **Sanitize** with boiling water or chemical disinfectants like chlorine-based solutions (food-safe concentration).
4. **Dry** the equipment in an inverted position to prevent recontamination.

Key equipment to clean regularly:

- Milk cans, pails, and strainers
- Milk machines and pipelines (if used)
- Weighing and measuring instruments
- Chilling tanks and storage vessels

Important tip: Never leave milk residue in utensils, as it encourages microbial growth and souring.

3. Simple Cooling and Preservation Techniques

Fresh milk should ideally be cooled to 4°C or below within 2 hours of milking to prevent bacterial multiplication. In rural or remote areas without access to advanced cooling systems, simple and cost-effective preservation methods are essential.

3.1 Natural Cooling Methods

a. Evaporative Cooling (Earthen Pot Method):

- Store milk in clay pots placed inside a larger pot filled with wet sand or water.
- Cover the pot with a wet cloth to facilitate evaporation.
- Ideal for short-term cooling where electricity is not available.

b. Cool Water Immersion:

- Place sealed milk containers in a tub of cool water or flowing stream.
- Prevents rapid temperature rise in warm climates.

3.2 Use of Ice

- Ice or ice packs can be placed around milk containers to lower temperature during transportation.

- Iceboxes or insulated crates are also helpful in preserving milk quality for several hours.

3.3 Use of Chilling Centers

- Bulk Milk Coolers (BMCs) are used in cooperative setups to chill milk at the village level.
- BMCs maintain milk at 4°C until it is collected for processing.
- Farmers are encouraged to deliver milk within 2–3 hours of milking to such centers.

3.4 Traditional Preservation Additives (for short-term use)

In certain rural practices, natural preservatives like turmeric or betel leaves are used. However, these should be used with caution and not as a substitute for proper hygiene and refrigeration.

Conclusion

Clean milk production is fundamental to ensuring public health, maintaining milk quality, and increasing the profitability of dairy enterprises. Adhering to hygienic practices during milking, maintaining personal and equipment cleanliness, and employing simple preservation methods can significantly reduce spoilage and contamination. With increasing consumer awareness and demand for safe dairy products, adopting clean milk production techniques is not just desirable but essential for the modern dairy farmer. Clean milk is not only safe milk—it is smart milk, valued by both markets and consumers alike.

4. Processing of Milk

Milk is a versatile and highly nutritious food that serves as the base for a wide range of value-added dairy products. Processing milk into curd, paneer, ghee, and khoa not only adds value but also extends its shelf life, reduces wastage, and creates new opportunities for small-scale rural entrepreneurship. This chapter explores the small-scale production of common dairy products, introduces low-cost processing equipment, and compares traditional and modern techniques used in milk processing.

---

1. Small-Scale Production of Dairy Products

1.1 Curd (Dahi)

Curd, or "dahi," is a fermented dairy product made by coagulating milk using bacterial cultures.

Steps for small-scale curd production:

1. **Boil milk** to 80–90°C and then cool it to 30–40°C.
2. **Add starter culture** (a spoon of previous day's curd or commercial culture) at about 1–2%.
3. **Mix thoroughly** and keep the vessel covered.

4. **Incubate** for 6–8 hours in a warm place without disturbance.
5. **Refrigerate** once curd is set to prevent over-acidification.

Key points:

- Use clean, boiled vessels to prevent contamination.
- Avoid stirring after inoculation.
- Can be packaged in earthen pots, plastic cups, or glass jars.

1.2 Paneer (Indian Cottage Cheese)

Paneer is a soft, fresh cheese made by curdling hot milk with food-grade acids.

Steps for small-scale paneer production:

1. **Boil fresh whole milk** (preferably buffalo milk for higher yield).
2. **Add lemon juice, vinegar, or citric acid** slowly to curdle the milk while stirring gently.
3. **Stop heating** once the whey separates clearly (light greenish liquid).
4. **Strain** the curds using a muslin cloth and drain the whey.
5. **Press** the curds underweight for 1–2 hours to form a solid block.

6. **Cut into cubes** and immerse in chilled water for firm texture.

Shelf life: 1–2 days at room temperature; 5–7 days when refrigerated.

1.3 Ghee (Clarified Butter)

Ghee is pure milk fat obtained by clarifying butter or cream.

Steps for small-scale ghee production:

1. **Collect cream** from milk or curd by skimming after refrigeration.
2. **Churn the cream** to separate butter.
3. **Melt and heat the butter** over low flame until the water evaporates and solids settle.
4. **Filter** the clear golden liquid (ghee) and store in clean containers.

Traditional method: Use earthen or metal pots and manual churning.
Shelf life: 6 months or more if stored in airtight containers.

1.4 Khoa (Mawa)

Khoa is a semi-solid dairy product used in Indian sweets.

Steps for khoa production:

1. **Boil full-fat milk** in a thick-bottomed pan.

2. **Stir continuously** on low flame to prevent burning.
3. **Scrape sides** to mix cream layers back into the milk.
4. **Continue heating** until a soft solid mass is formed.
5. **Cool and store** for use in sweets like gulab jamun or peda.

Yield: ~20–25% of initial milk volume.

---

2. Low-Cost Processing Equipment Overview

Small-scale dairy entrepreneurs or rural households can use low-cost and locally available tools for milk processing. Below is a summary of useful equipment:

Equipment	**Purpose**	**Approx Cost**	**Features**
Milk boiling kettle	Boiling and pasteurization	₹1,500–₹3,000	Stainless steel; manual operation
Muslin cloth	Filtration and straining	₹100–₹200	Reusable; food-grade cotton

Equipment	Purpose	Approx Cost	Features
Manual cream separator	Cream extraction for ghee	₹5,000–₹10,000	Hand-operated; small capacity
Paneer press	Paneer shaping and compacting	₹1,500–₹3,000	Manual with weight or screw mechanism
Butter churner	Separates butter from cream	₹1,000–₹5,000	Available in hand, electric, and motorized
Khoya pan (karahi)	Evaporation of milk for khoa	₹2,000–₹5,000	Thick bottom; avoids scorching
Ghee boiler	Heating butter to extract ghee	₹3,000–₹6,000	Direct heat or steam jacketed

Note: Prices may vary based on location, material quality, and capacity.

---

3. Traditional vs Modern Techniques

Traditional Techniques

Advantages:

- Low cost and suitable for small-scale, rural setups.
- Uses locally available materials and fuels (wood, dung cakes).
- Retains unique flavour and texture of products like ghee and curd.

Limitations:

- Labor-intensive and time-consuming.
- Risk of contamination due to open-air processing.
- Inconsistent product quality and yield.

Modern Techniques

Examples:

- Pasteurizers for safe milk processing.
- Paneer and khoa making machines with thermostatic control.
- Electric cream separators and butter churners.

Advantages:

- Hygienic and standardized processing.
- Higher yield and consistency.
- Time-saving and suitable for scaling up.

Limitations:

- Higher initial investment.
- Requires electricity or diesel.

- May not replicate traditional taste in some products.

Conclusion

Milk processing at the small scale is a practical and profitable avenue for rural households and budding entrepreneurs. With basic knowledge and low-cost equipment, producers can convert surplus milk into valuable products like curd, paneer, ghee, and khoa. A blend of traditional knowledge and modern tools can enhance hygiene, improve shelf life, and cater to both local and urban markets. Promoting milk processing not only reduces wastage but also strengthens rural livelihoods and supports the broader dairy ecosystem.

MILK
MILK
MILK

5. Value Addition and Marketing in the Dairy Sector

The dairy sector occupies a vital position within global agriculture, providing a significant source of nutrition and livelihood for millions. However, the traditional model of simply producing and selling raw milk is increasingly insufficient in today's dynamic and competitive market. To ensure sustainability, enhance profitability, and cater to evolving consumer demands, stakeholders in the dairy industry must prioritize value addition and implement effective marketing strategies. This chapter delves into the critical aspects of transforming raw milk into a diverse portfolio of value-added products and strategically positioning them in the marketplace. We will explore the various processes involved in value addition, analyze key marketing concepts and strategies, and consider the specific context of emerging economies, with a focus on the roles of cooperatives and private enterprises.

1. The Economic Rationale for Value Addition

Value addition refers to the process of enhancing the worth of a raw commodity, in this case, raw milk, by transforming it into a more desirable product. This transformation goes beyond basic processing; it encompasses activities that modify the physical form, improve quality, extend shelf life, enhance packaging, or add specific attributes to the original product. The economic rationale for value addition in the dairy sector is compelling:

- **Increased Income and Profitability:** Raw milk is often characterized by low prices and fluctuating demand. Value addition allows producers and processors to capture a greater share of the consumer's expenditure by offering products with higher price points and profit margins.
- **Market Diversification and Risk Mitigation:** Relying solely on raw milk sales exposes dairy businesses to market volatility and price fluctuations. A diversified portfolio of value-added products, targeting different consumer segments, can buffer against these risks and create more stable revenue streams.
- **Meeting Consumer Needs and Preferences:** Modern consumers are increasingly demanding convenience, variety, and specific nutritional benefits from their food choices. Value addition enables the dairy sector to cater to these diverse preferences with products like ready-to-drink flavored milk, on-the-go yogurt snacks, and fortified milk powders.
- **Extension of Shelf Life and Reduction of Waste:** Raw milk is highly perishable, limiting

its distribution range and leading to significant wastage. Processing milk into products like UHT milk, cheese, and milk powder dramatically extends its shelf life, reduces spoilage, and allows access to more distant markets.

- **Creation of Employment Opportunities:** Value addition activities, such as processing, packaging, and marketing, create new employment opportunities throughout the dairy supply chain, contributing to economic growth and rural development.
- **Enhanced Competitiveness:** In a globalized market, value addition is essential for dairy producers and processors to differentiate their products and compete effectively with both domestic and international players.

2. Technological Processes in Dairy Value Addition:

The transformation of raw milk into value-added products involves a range of technological processes, each designed to achieve specific objectives:

- **Primary Processing:** These processes form the foundation for further value addition:
    - **Cleaning and Filtration:** Removing impurities and foreign matter from raw milk to ensure hygiene and product quality.

    - **Cooling:** Rapidly reducing the temperature of raw milk to inhibit bacterial growth and preserve its freshness.
    - **Standardization:** Adjusting the fat content of milk to meet specific product requirements.
- **Heat Treatment:** A critical step in ensuring milk safety and extending shelf life:
    - **Pasteurization:** Heating milk to a specific temperature (e.g., 72°C for 15 seconds) to kill pathogenic bacteria while preserving its nutritional value. This extends shelf life for a few days under refrigeration.
    - **Ultra-High Temperature (UHT) Processing:** Heating milk to very high temperatures (e.g., 135-150°C) for a short duration (2-4 seconds), followed by aseptic packaging. UHT processing results in shelf-stable milk that can be stored at room temperature for several months.
- **Fermentation:** Utilizing beneficial microorganisms to transform milk into cultured dairy products:
    - **Yogurt Production:** Inoculating milk with specific strains of bacteria (e.g.,

Lactobacillus and *Streptococcus*) to produce a thick, tangy product.

- **Cheese Making:** Adding rennet or acid to coagulate milk, separating the curd from the whey, and then subjecting the curd to various processing and aging techniques to create a wide variety of cheese types.
- **Dahi (Curd) Production:** A traditional Indian fermented milk product produced by inoculating warm milk with a starter culture containing beneficial bacteria.

- **Separation and Concentration:** Modifying the composition of milk to create different products:
    - **Cream Separation:** Separating the fat-rich portion of milk to produce cream, which can be further processed into butter.
    - **Butter Production:** Churning cream until the fat globules coalesce, separating the butter from the buttermilk.
    - **Ghee (Clarified Butter) Production:** Heating butter to remove moisture and milk solids, resulting in a shelf-stable, golden-yellow product widely used in Indian cooking.
    - **Milk Powder Production:** Removing water from milk through spray drying or other methods to create a shelf-stable

powder, which can be reconstituted into liquid milk or used as an ingredient in other products.

- **Formulation and Blending:** Combining milk or milk components with other ingredients to create novel or enhanced products:
    - **Flavored Milk Production:** Adding flavors, sweeteners, and sometimes colorings to milk to appeal to specific consumer segments, particularly children.
    - **Fortified Milk Production:** Adding vitamins and minerals (e.g., vitamin D, calcium) to milk to enhance its nutritional value.
    - **Dairy Desserts:** Combining milk with sugar, stabilizers, and flavorings to create products like ice cream, puddings, and custards.
- **Packaging:** Protecting the product, extending shelf life, and enhancing consumer appeal:
    - Aseptic packaging
    - Modified Atmosphere packaging
    - Various sizes and materials.

3. Marketing Strategies in the Dairy Sector:

Effective marketing is essential to communicate the value of dairy products, build brand loyalty, and reach target consumers. Key marketing strategies include:

- **Market Research:** Understanding consumer preferences, buying habits, and needs is crucial for developing products that meet market demand. Methods include surveys, focus groups, and analyzing sales data.
- **Target Market Identification:** Identifying specific groups of consumers (e.g., children, health-conscious adults, elderly) with distinct needs and preferences allows for targeted marketing campaigns.
- **Product Development and Innovation:** Creating new and differentiated products to cater to evolving consumer tastes. This includes exploring new flavors, formats, and health benefits (e.g., probiotic dairy products, lactose-free milk).
- **Branding:** Creating a strong brand identity that resonates with consumers and differentiates the product from competitors. Key elements include a memorable brand name, logo, packaging design, and brand messaging. Brands like Amul, renowned for quality and consistency, have mastered this.

- **Pricing Strategies:** Setting prices that are competitive yet allow for profitability, considering production costs, perceived value, and competitor pricing. Strategies include cost-plus pricing, value-based pricing, and competitive pricing.
- **Distribution Channels:** Selecting the most efficient and effective channels to reach target consumers. Options include:
    - Direct Sales: Farm-to-consumer sales, online orders, and home delivery.
    - Retail Channels: Supermarkets, grocery stores, convenience stores.
    - Institutional Sales: Supplying to hotels, restaurants, and catering services.
    - E-commerce: Selling dairy products online, often with delivery services.
- **Promotion and Advertising:** Communicating product information and benefits to target consumers to create awareness, interest, and purchase intent. Methods include:
    - Advertising: Using paid media, such as television, radio, print, and online platforms, to reach a broad audience.
    - Sales Promotion: Offering short-term incentives, such as discounts, coupons, and free samples, to encourage trial and purchase.

- Public Relations: Building positive relationships with the media and the public to enhance brand image and credibility.
- Digital Marketing: Utilizing online platforms, such as social media, search engines, and email, to reach and engage with consumers.
- Content Marketing: Creating valuable and informative content, such as blog posts, videos, and articles, to attract and engage potential customers.

- **Consumer Relationship Management (CRM):** Building long-term relationships with customers through personalized communication, loyalty programs, and excellent customer service.
- **Point-of-Sale Marketing:** Influencing purchase decisions at the point of sale through attractive displays, product placement, and promotional materials.
- **Sustainable Marketing:** Emphasizing ethical and environmentally responsible practices in production, processing, and distribution.

4. Case Study: The Amul Model

The Amul cooperative in India provides a compelling example of successful value addition and marketing in the dairy sector. Amul has transformed the lives of millions of dairy farmers and become a national brand through a combination of:

- **Empowering Farmers:** A cooperative structure that ensures farmers receive a fair price for their milk and participate in the governance of the organization.
- **Efficient Milk Procurement Network:** A well-organized network for collecting milk from thousands of villages, ensuring quality and timeliness.
- **Wide Product Range:** A diverse portfolio of value-added products, including milk powder, cheese, butter, ghee, ice cream, and more, catering to different consumer segments.
- **Strong Branding and Marketing:** A consistent and effective brand image, memorable advertising campaigns, and a focus on quality and affordability.
- **Extensive Distribution Network:** A vast network of distributors and retailers ensures that Amul products are readily available to consumers across India.

5. Challenges and Opportunities in Emerging Economies:

In emerging economies, the dairy sector faces both unique challenges and significant opportunities in terms of value addition and marketing:

- **Infrastructure Constraints:** Inadequate cold chain infrastructure, poor transportation networks, and unreliable electricity supply can hinder the development of value-added dairy products and efficient distribution.
- **Low Purchasing Power:** A large segment of the population may have limited purchasing power, making it challenging to market premium, value-added products.
- **Lack of Awareness:** Consumers in some areas may have limited awareness of the nutritional benefits of milk and dairy products, as well as the variety of value-added options available.
- **Competition from Informal Sector:** In many emerging economies, a significant portion of the dairy market is served by the informal sector, which may offer lower-priced, unregulated products.
- **Opportunities:**
    - **Growing Urbanization and Middle Class:** Rising incomes and increasing urbanization are driving demand for processed and packaged dairy products.
    - **Government Support:** Many governments are promoting the development of the dairy sector through subsidies, infrastructure investments, and policies that encourage value addition.

- **Technological Advancements:** Affordable and appropriate technologies are becoming increasingly available to help small and medium-sized enterprises (SMEs) engage in value addition.
- **Potential for Export:** Some emerging economies have the potential to become exporters of value-added dairy products to regional and international markets.

Recommendations for Success:

To maximize the potential of value addition and marketing in the dairy sector, particularly in emerging economies, the following recommendations are crucial:

- **Investing in Infrastructure:** Governments and private sector entities should prioritize investments in cold chain facilities, transportation networks, and other infrastructure to support the efficient processing, distribution, and storage of dairy products.
- **Capacity Building:** Providing training and technical assistance to dairy farmers, processors, and marketers to improve their skills and knowledge in value addition techniques and marketing strategies.
- **Supporting SMEs:** Offering financial assistance, access to technology, and business development services to encourage the growth of small and medium-sized dairy enterprises.

- **Promoting Public-Private Partnerships:** Fostering collaboration between government, private sector, and non-governmental organizations to leverage resources, expertise, and innovation in the dairy sector.
- **Raising Consumer Awareness:** Conducting public education campaigns to promote the nutritional benefits of milk and dairy products and to increase consumer demand for value-added options.
- **Enhancing Quality and Safety Standards:** Implementing and enforcing stringent quality and safety standards to ensure the production of safe and high-quality dairy products, building consumer trust.
- **Developing Sustainable Practices:** Promote environmentally sound practices throughout the dairy sector.
- **Market Information Systems:** Provide market data to farmers and processors.

Conclusion:

Value addition and effective marketing are essential for the sustainable growth and prosperity of the dairy sector in both developed and emerging economies. By transforming raw milk into a diverse range of value-added products and reaching target consumers through strategic marketing initiatives, stakeholders can enhance profitability, reduce waste, meet evolving consumer demands, and contribute to economic development. By addressing the challenges and capitalizing on the opportunities, the dairy sector can continue to play a crucial role in providing nutritious food, generating income, and improving livelihoods worldwide. The success of this endeavor depends on embracing innovation, fostering collaboration, and adopting a market-oriented approach that prioritizes consumer needs and preferences.

6. Government Support & Entrepreneurships in the Dairy Sector

India's dairy sector is not only the largest in the world but also deeply rooted in the rural economy. For states like **Jharkhand**, where agriculture and livestock are central to rural livelihoods, dairy entrepreneurship offers significant opportunities for employment, income generation, and nutrition enhancement. To support this, the government has launched various schemes and initiatives. In this chapter, we explore major government schemes like **DEDS**, **Rashtriya Gokul Mission**, and **NABARD** assistance, examine the role of **cooperatives and Self-Help Groups (SHGs)**, and provide a practical guide on starting a **small-scale dairy unit in Jharkhand**.

---

1. Government Schemes Supporting Dairy Entrepreneurship

Dairy farming plays a crucial role in the rural economy of many countries, providing livelihoods and contributing to food security. Recognizing its potential for economic growth and social development, governments worldwide have implemented various schemes and initiatives to promote dairy entrepreneurship. These programs aim to provide financial assistance, technical guidance, and infrastructure support to individuals and organizations involved in dairy production, processing, and marketing. This chapter examines the key government schemes designed to foster dairy entrepreneurship, with a particular focus on the Indian context.

The Importance of Government Support for Dairy Entrepreneurship:

Dairy farming often requires significant upfront investment in cattle, infrastructure, and equipment. Many aspiring entrepreneurs, especially in developing economies, lack the financial resources and technical expertise to establish and operate successful dairy businesses. Government support is crucial for:

- **Reducing Financial Barriers:** Providing access to affordable credit, subsidies, and grants can alleviate the financial burden on entrepreneurs and encourage investment in the dairy sector.
- **Enhancing Technical Skills:** Training programs, workshops, and extension services can equip entrepreneurs with the knowledge and skills needed to adopt modern dairy farming practices, improve productivity, and ensure quality.
- **Developing Infrastructure:** Government initiatives can facilitate the development of essential infrastructure, such as milk collection centers, chilling plants, and processing facilities,

which are vital for the growth of the dairy industry.

- **Promoting Market Linkages:** Connecting dairy entrepreneurs with markets, both local and regional, can help them sell their products at remunerative prices and expand their businesses.
- **Encouraging Innovation:** Government support for research and development can lead to the adoption of new technologies and practices that improve efficiency, reduce costs, and enhance the competitiveness of the dairy sector.
- **Creating Employment Opportunities:** By promoting dairy entrepreneurship, governments can help generate employment opportunities, particularly in rural areas, and contribute to poverty reduction.

Key Government Schemes for Dairy Entrepreneurship:

Several countries have implemented schemes to support dairy entrepreneurship. Here, we will look at some prominent schemes, with a focus on India:

India:

India is the world's largest milk producer, and the government has played a significant role in the development of its dairy sector. Several schemes and initiatives have been launched to promote dairy entrepreneurship, including:

- **National Programme for Dairy Development (NPDD):** The NPDD is a central sector scheme implemented by the Department of Animal Husbandry and Dairying. It aims to enhance milk production, procurement, processing, and marketing. The scheme has two components:
    - **Component A:** Focuses on creating and strengthening infrastructure for quality milk testing and chilling.
    - **Component B:** Promotes dairying through cooperatives, increasing farmers' access to organized markets, upgrading processing facilities, and enhancing the capacity of producer-owned institutions.
- **Dairy Infrastructure Development Fund (DIDF):** DIDF aims to modernize milk processing plants and establish infrastructure for milk processing and value addition. It provides financial assistance to eligible entities, including state dairy federations, milk unions, and producer companies. The scheme provides subsidized loans to assist in the modernization and expansion of dairy processing facilities.
- **Animal Husbandry Infrastructure Development Fund (AHIDF):** AHIDF incentivizes investments in the establishment of dairy processing and value addition infrastructure, meat processing, animal feed plants, and other related activities. It provides

financial assistance to private companies, entrepreneurs, and cooperatives.

- **Rashtriya Gokul Mission (RGM):** RGM focuses on the development and conservation of indigenous bovine breeds to improve milk productivity. It supports the establishment of integrated cattle development centers, strengthening breeding infrastructure, and promoting indigenous cattle rearing.
- **National Livestock Mission (NLM):** The NLM aims to promote sustainable livestock development, including dairy, through various interventions. It provides support for breed improvement, feed and fodder development, healthcare, and infrastructure development.
- **Supporting Dairy Cooperatives and Farmer Producer Organizations (SDCFPO):** This scheme assists dairy cooperatives and farmer producer organizations by providing working capital loans to help them during periods of market disruption or natural calamities.

Other Countries:

Many other countries have also implemented programs to support dairy entrepreneurship, tailored to their specific contexts. These may include:

- **European Union:** The EU's Common Agricultural Policy (CAP) provides support to dairy farmers through various measures, including direct payments, market interventions, and rural development programs. These programs often support investments in farm modernization, diversification, and value addition.

- **United States:** The US Department of Agriculture (USDA) offers several programs to support dairy farmers, including loan programs, grant programs, and technical assistance. These programs aim to improve farm profitability, promote sustainable practices, and support market development.
- **New Zealand:** New Zealand's dairy industry is largely driven by market forces, but the government provides support through research and development, biosecurity measures, and trade negotiations. Organizations like DairyNZ also provide resources and support to dairy farmers.
- **Australia:** Dairy Australia supports dairy farmers through research and development.

2. NABARD's Role in Dairy Development in India:

The National Bank for Agriculture and Rural Development (NABARD) plays a crucial role in promoting dairy entrepreneurship in India. NABARD provides refinance to banks for lending to dairy farmers and entrepreneurs, supports the development of dairy infrastructure, and implements various dairy-related schemes. Its initiatives aim to:

- Facilitate credit flow to the dairy sector.
- Promote the establishment of modern dairy farms.
- Support the development of milk processing and marketing infrastructure.
- Enhance the technical skills of dairy farmers and entrepreneurs.
- Encourage the formation of dairy cooperatives and producer organizations.

Challenges and Opportunities:

Despite the various government schemes and initiatives, dairy entrepreneurs still face several challenges, including:

- **Limited Access to Credit:** Many smallholders dairy farmers and entrepreneurs struggle to access affordable credit from formal financial institutions.
- **Inadequate Infrastructure:** The lack of proper cold chain facilities, transportation networks, and processing units can hinder the growth of dairy businesses.
- **Technical Knowledge Gap:** Many dairy farmers lack the knowledge and skills needed to adopt modern practices and improve productivity.

- **Market Volatility:** Fluctuations in milk prices and market demand can create uncertainty for dairy entrepreneurs.
- **Competition:** Dairy entrepreneurs face competition from established players, both in the organized and unorganized sectors.

However, there are also significant opportunities for growth and development in the dairy sector:

- **Growing Demand:** The demand for milk and dairy products is increasing due to rising incomes, urbanization, and changing dietary patterns.
- **Value Addition:** There is significant potential for dairy entrepreneurs to increase their income by processing milk into value-added products, such as cheese, yogurt, and ice cream.
- **Technological Advancements:** New technologies, such as improved cattle breeds, modern milking equipment, and efficient processing techniques, can help dairy entrepreneurs improve productivity and reduce costs.
- **Government Support:** Continued government support through various schemes and initiatives can create a favorable environment for dairy entrepreneurship.

Conclusion:

Government schemes and initiatives play a vital role in promoting dairy entrepreneurship by addressing the challenges faced by entrepreneurs and creating opportunities for growth. These programs provide financial assistance, technical guidance, and infrastructure support, enabling individuals and organizations to establish and operate successful dairy businesses. In countries like India, the government's focus on dairy development has contributed significantly to the growth of the sector and improved the livelihoods of millions of people. To ensure the continued success of dairy entrepreneurship, governments need to continuously evaluate and improve their support mechanisms, address emerging challenges, and capitalize on the opportunities presented by the evolving market and technological landscape.

3. Key Government Schemes for Dairy Entrepreneurship

Dairy entrepreneurship plays a vital role in rural development and economic growth. The Indian government has launched several schemes to support and promote dairy farming. Here's a detailed look at key government schemes:

3.1. National Livestock Mission (NLM)

Launched by: Ministry of Fisheries, Animal Husbandry and Dairying

Objectives:

- To promote entrepreneurship in livestock sector.
- To increase productivity of livestock.
- To enhance availability of quality feed and fodder.

Key Features:

- Sub-missions include Livestock Development, Feed and Fodder Development, and Skill Development & Technology Transfer.
- Financial assistance provided for setting up dairy units.
- Focus on breed improvement and disease control.

Benefits:

- Increased income for dairy farmers.
- Employment generation in rural areas.
- Improved livestock health and productivity.

Eligibility:

- Individual farmers, self-help groups, cooperatives, and entrepreneurs involved in dairy activities.

3.2. Dairy Entrepreneurship Development Scheme (DEDS)

Launched by: **National Bank for Agriculture and Rural Development (NABARD)**

Objectives:

- To generate self-employment opportunities in the dairy sector.
- To provide infrastructure for milk production, procurement, and processing.
- To upgrade traditional dairy farming practices.

Key Features:

- Provides financial assistance in the form of subsidies and loans.
- Focuses on small and marginal farmers.
- Supports establishment of small dairy farms, milk chilling units, and dairy product processing units.

Benefits:

- Easy access to credit for dairy entrepreneurs.
- Modernization of dairy farming practices.
- Enhanced market access for dairy products.

Eligibility:

- Individual entrepreneurs, farmers, NGOs, self-help groups, and companies can apply.

3.3. Rashtriya Gokul Mission

Launched by: Ministry of Fisheries, Animal Husbandry and Dairying

Objectives:

- To conserve and develop indigenous bovine breeds.
- To enhance milk production and productivity.
- To upgrade bovine breeding infrastructure.

Key Features:

- Focus on genetic improvement of indigenous cattle breeds.
- Establishment of integrated indigenous cattle centers (Gokul Grams).

- Provides support for bull production and distribution.

Benefits:

- Increased availability of high-yielding indigenous breeds.
- Improved milk production efficiency.
- Conservation of valuable genetic resources.

Eligibility:

- Breeders' societies, NGOs, and other organizations involved in cattle development.

3.4. Animal Husbandry Infrastructure Development Fund (AHIDF)

Launched by: Government of India

Objectives:

- To incentivize investments in animal husbandry infrastructure.
- To promote private sector participation in dairy processing and value addition.
- To create employment opportunities in the rural sector.

Key Features:

- Provides interest subvention for eligible borrowers.
- Supports establishment of dairy processing plants, meat processing units, and animal feed plants.
- Encourages export-oriented units.

Benefits:

- Attracts private investment in dairy infrastructure.
- Increased processing capacity for dairy products.
- Better price realization for farmers.

Eligibility:

- Private entrepreneurs, farmer producer organizations, and MSMEs involved in animal husbandry sector.

3.5. Jharkhand State-Specific Initiatives

While details on exclusively Jharkhand-run dairy schemes can be limited, the state government actively works to promote dairy through:

- **Jharkhand Milk Federation (JMF):** The state has been working to strengthen the JMF to support dairy farmers, improve milk procurement, and market dairy products under the "Medha" brand. Collaborations with the National Dairy Development Board (NDDB) are crucial in this effort.

- **Incentives for Milk Producers:** The Jharkhand government has introduced incentive schemes to encourage milk producers to supply to state-owned dairies like Medha Dairy. This helps to ensure a stable supply of milk for processing and distribution.
- **Support for Infrastructure Development:** The state government, in conjunction with central schemes, supports the development of dairy infrastructure, including chilling units, processing plants, and collection centers.
- **Training and Capacity Building:** Jharkhand also emphasizes training programs for dairy farmers to improve their practices, enhance productivity, and adopt modern techniques.

Where to Find the Latest Information

For the most current and detailed information on specific schemes in Jharkhand, it's advisable to check these resources:

- **Department of Animal Husbandry, Jharkhand:** This state government department will have the latest details on state-specific programs.

- **Jharkhand Milk Federation (JMF):** JMF can provide information on milk procurement policies, support to farmers, and related schemes.
- **NABARD (National Bank for Agriculture and Rural Development):** NABARD plays a significant role in implementing many dairy development schemes and can offer details on financial assistance.

---

4. How to Start a Small-Scale Dairy Unit in Jharkhand

Starting a dairy business in Jharkhand can be highly rewarding if planned and executed well. Below is a step-by-step guide tailored to local conditions.

Step 1: Planning the Business

- **Decide scale**: Start with 2–10 cows or buffaloes.
- **Choose breed**: Crossbred Jersey, Holstein Friesian, or Indigenous breeds like Gir or Sahiwal.
- **Location**: Choose a place near fodder, water, and market.
- **Build shed**: Proper ventilation, drainage, and protection from heat/rain.
- **Feed plan**: green fodder, dry fodder, concentrate, and clean water.

Step 2: Financial Planning

- **Estimate costs**: Animal purchase, shed construction, feed, labor, equipment.
- **Approach bank**: Apply for a loan under DEDS or other schemes.
- **Apply for subsidy**: Route application through NABARD or animal husbandry department.

Step 3: Registration and Training

- **Register unit** with Panchayat or Livestock department.
- **Get FSSAI license** if processing or selling packaged milk.
- **Attend training** under schemes like RKVY, Rashtriya Gokul Mission, or KVK programs.

Step 4: Procurement and Setup

- **Buy healthy animals** from reputed sources with vet certification.
- **Set up milking equipment**, chaff cutters, water supply.
- **Keep records** for feeding, health, breeding, and milk output.

Step 5: Milk Sale and Marketing

- Sell milk to:
    - Local consumers
    - Cooperatives like *Medha Dairy*
    - Bulk buyers (sweet shops, hotels)

- Explore value addition: curd, paneer, ghee, lassi.
- Use **branding and packaging** for direct retail sales.

Conclusion

The dairy sector in Jharkhand holds immense potential for rural development and employment. With targeted support from government schemes like DEDS, Rashtriya Gokul Mission, and NABARD, coupled with the institutional strength of cooperatives and SHGs, small-scale dairy entrepreneurship can thrive. By leveraging financial aid, technical training, and market linkages, rural youth and women can build sustainable dairy businesses. Jharkhand's climate, natural resources, and community-driven models provide a fertile ground for a dairy revolution that is inclusive, profitable, and enduring.

5. Practical

1. Dairy Processing Equipment – Principles, Working & Design

In the dairy industry, maintaining quality and safety is critical. Various mechanical and thermal equipment help process milk efficiently while retaining its nutritional value. This chapter discusses the **principle, working, and design** of five essential dairy processing instruments:

1. Pasteuriser
2. Homogenizer
3. Freezer
4. Cream Separator
5. Milk Sampling Equipment

---

1. Pasteuriser

Principle:

Pasteurisation is the process of **heating milk to a specific temperature for a set period** to kill pathogenic microorganisms without altering its nutritional value. The principle is based on **thermal inactivation** of microbes.

Working:

Pasteurisation can be done using different methods:

- **Low-Temperature Long Time (LTLT):** 63°C for 30 minutes
- **High-Temperature Short Time (HTST):** 72°C for 15 seconds
- **Ultra-High Temperature (UHT):** 135°C for 2–5 seconds

HTST Pasteurizer (Plate Type):

1. Raw milk is preheated and passed through **plate heat exchangers (PHE)**.
2. Milk flows between alternate plates with hot water or steam on the other side.
3. It reaches 72°C, held for 15 seconds in a **holding tube**.
4. Then cooled to below 4°C using chilled water or glycol.

Design:

- **Heat exchanger plates:** Stainless steel with corrugated surfaces
- **Holding tube:** Ensures residence time
- **Flow diversion valve:** Diverts improperly pasteurized milk
- **Thermal sensors & controllers:** Monitor temperature

2. Homogenizer

Principle:

Homogenization is the mechanical process of breaking down **fat globules in milk** into smaller sizes to prevent cream separation and ensure uniform texture. It works on **shear force and turbulence**.

Working:

1. Milk is pumped under high pressure (1500–2500 psi) into a **homogenizing valve**.
2. The milk passes through a narrow gap at high speed.
3. Sudden pressure drops and impact break fat globules into tiny, uniform particles (<2 microns).
4. Homogenized milk exits with improved stability and mouthfeel.

Design:

- **Plunger pump**: Provides required pressure
- **Homogenizing valve**: Made of stainless steel with narrow orifice
- **Pressure gauge**: Ensures consistent performance
- **Cooling jacket**: Maintains milk temperature

---

3. Freezer

Principle:

A freezer removes heat from dairy products using the principle of **refrigeration**, typically based on **vapor compression cycle**. This is essential for producing frozen products like **ice cream**.

Working (Batch or Continuous Freezer for Ice Cream):

1. Mixture is fed into a freezing barrel.
2. Ammonia or Freon circulates around the barrel and removes heat.
3. The product is continuously scraped off the freezing surface by **rotating blades** to prevent crystallization.
4. Air is incorporated during freezing for fluffiness (overrun).
5. Semi-frozen product is filled into molds or containers.

Design:

- **Insulated tank**: Stainless steel barrel with refrigeration coils
- **Agitator/scraper blades**: Prevent buildup and ensure mixing
- **Compressor unit**: Circulates refrigerant (ammonia/Freon)
- **Expansion valve**: Controls refrigerant flow

4. Cream Separator

Principle:

Cream separation is based on the **difference in density** between milk and cream (fat). Under centrifugal force, heavier skim milk is pushed outward, and lighter cream moves inward.

Working:

1. Milk enters a rapidly rotating bowl (5,000–10,000 RPM).
2. The **centrifugal force** separates fat from the skim milk.
3. Separated cream and skim milk exit through different outlets.
4. Flow rates and fat content can be adjusted using regulating screws.

Design:

- **Bowl with conical discs**: Stainless steel discs create thin milk films for faster separation
- **Inlet/outlet pipes**: For milk, cream, and skim milk
- **Motor and shaft**: Provide high-speed rotation
- **Base frame and adjustment knob**: Set fat content in cream

---

5. Milk Sampling Equipment

Principle:

Milk sampling is based on the **representative sampling principle**, where a small sample accurately reflects the entire batch's quality and composition.

Working:

1. Before sampling, milk is thoroughly mixed to ensure uniformity.
2. **Milk samplers or dippers** are used to collect samples from various depths.
3. In-line or automatic samplers collect milk from pipelines in real time.

Tests typically conducted on samples include:

- Fat and SNF content
- Adulteration tests
- Microbial load
- pH and temperature

Design:

- **Milk sampling dipper**: Stainless steel, 100–200 ml capacity
- **Lactoscan inlet or milk valve samplers**: Attached to tanks or pipelines
- **Sample bottles**: Food-grade plastic or glass, with labels

- **Sterilizer or sanitizer container**: To disinfect equipment between uses

---

Conclusion

Efficient dairy processing depends heavily on well-designed equipment that ensures product safety, quality, and shelf life. Understanding the **principle, working, and design** of pasteurisers, homogenizers, freezers, cream separators, and sampling tools is essential for dairy entrepreneurs, technicians, and quality managers. Adopting appropriate technology helps not only in compliance with standards but also in improving profitability and consumer satisfaction in the dairy sector.

2. Determine the specific gravity of milk

---

1. Materials and Methods

Materials Required:

- Clean lactometer
- Graduated measuring cylinder or lactometer jar (500 ml)
- Milk sample (fresh/raw)
- Thermometer
- Stirrer

---

2. Principle

Specific gravity is the **ratio of the density of milk to the density of water** at a standard temperature (usually 27°C in India).
The **lactometer** floats higher in denser milk and sinks in diluted or low-density milk. The reading obtained is corrected for temperature deviation from the standard.

---

3. Methodology

1. **Take about 250 ml of milk** in the lactometer jar.
2. Ensure the milk is **free of froth** and at **room temperature** (preferably 27°C).

3. Gently lower the **lactometer into the milk** until it floats freely.
4. Record the **lactometer reading (LR)** at the bottom of the meniscus.
5. Note the **temperature** of the milk using a thermometer.
6. Apply the **temperature correction** if required:
   - Add 0.2 to the LR for every 1°C **above** 27°C
   - Subtract 0.2 from the LR for every 1°C **below** 27°C

Formula to calculate Specific Gravity:

$$Specific\ Gravity\ (SG) = \frac{\textbf{Corrected LR}}{\textbf{1000}} + 1$$

---

4. Observation

Parameter	**Value**
Lactometer Reading (LR)	30
Milk Temperature	29°C
Correction (+0.4)	30 + 0.4 = 30.4
Specific Gravity	1.0304

---

5. Conclusion

The specific gravity of the milk sample was found to be **1.0304**, which lies within the **normal range for**

cow/buffalo milk (1.028 – 1.032). This indicates that the milk is likely **pure and not adulterated with water**.

This test is a simple yet effective method for **initial quality screening** of milk at collection centers or small dairy units.

3. Determine the fat content in milk

---

1. Materials and Methods

Materials Required:

- Milk sample
- Gerber butyrometer (10 ml)
- Pipette (10.75 ml)
- Sulphuric acid (specific gravity 1.815)
- Amyl alcohol (isoamyl alcohol)
- Gerber centrifuge
- Water bath (65°C)
- Stopper and lock wrench
- Safety gloves and goggles

---

2. Principle

The **Gerber method** works on the principle that **sulphuric acid dissolves proteins and releases fat**, which is then separated by centrifugation. The fat layer settles at the top of the butyrometer and is **measured directly as a percentage** on the calibrated scale.

---

3. Methodology

1. **Add 10 ml of sulphuric acid** carefully to the Gerber butyrometer.

2. Add **11 ml of well-mixed milk sample** using a pipette.
3. Add **1 ml of amyl alcohol.**
4. Insert the stopper and **shake the butyrometer gently** until the contents mix uniformly.
5. Place the butyrometer in the **Gerber centrifuge** and centrifuge for **5 minutes at 1100–1200 rpm**.
6. Remove and transfer the butyrometer to a **water bath at 65°C for 5 minutes.**
7. Read the **fat content** directly from the calibrated scale of the butyrometer.

---

4. Observation

Parameter	Value
Volume of milk used	11 ml
Sulphuric acid used	10 ml
Amyl alcohol used	1 ml
Fat reading on butyrometer	4.5%

---

5. Conclusion

The **fat content of the milk sample is 4.5%**, which is within the expected range for buffalo milk and high-fat cow milk. This indicates that the milk is of **good quality** and suitable for **consumption or processing** into products like ghee, butter, or cheese.

The Gerber method is a **simple, quick, and reliable technique** widely used in the dairy industry for routine fat analysis.

4. Determine the Solid-Not-Fat (SNF) content in a milk

---

1. Materials and Methods

Materials Required:

- Milk sample
- Lactometer
- Thermometer
- Measuring cylinder or lactometer jar
- Stirrer
- Calculator

---

2. Principle

SNF content includes **proteins, lactose, minerals, and vitamins** present in milk excluding fat. The **SNF content is calculated indirectly** using the **corrected lactometer reading (CLR)** and **fat percentage** obtained (e.g., from Gerber method) with an empirical formula.

---

3. Methodology

1. Pour the milk sample into a **lactometer jar** and let it come to room temperature.
2. Record the **lactometer reading (LR)** at eye level.

3. Measure the **temperature of the milk** using a thermometer.
4. Apply the **temperature correction**:
    - Add 0.2 to LR for each °C above 27°C
    - Subtract 0.2 for each °C below 27°C

$$Corrected\ LR\ (CLR) = LR\ \pm Temp\ Correction$$

5. Determine the **fat %** (from Gerber test or assumed).
6. Calculate the **SNF using the formula**:

$$SNF = \frac{CLR}{4} + (0.25\ x\ Fat) + 0.44$$

---

4. Observation

Parameter	**Value**
Lactometer Reading (LR)	30
Temperature of milk	28°C
Temperature Correction	+0.2
Corrected LR (CLR)	30.2
Fat % (from Gerber method)	4.5%

$$\text{SNF (calculated)} = \frac{30.2}{4} + (0.25 \times 4.5) + 0.44$$

$$= 7.55 + 1.125 = 9.12\%$$

---

5. Conclusion

The **SNF content of the milk sample is 9.12%**, which falls within the **normal range (8.5–9.5%)** for cow/buffalo milk. This suggests that the milk is of **good quality and not adulterated**.

SNF determination is essential in **pricing milk at collection centers**, ensuring **nutritional quality**, and **detecting dilution or skimming**.

5. Determination of Total Solids (TS) Content of Milk

---

1. Aim

To determine the **Total Solids (TS)** content in a milk sample, which includes both **fat and solid-not-fat (SNF)** components.

---

2. Materials and Methods

Materials Required:

- Milk sample
- Lactometer
- Thermometer
- Graduated cylinder or lactometer jar
- Gerber butyrometer (for fat % determination)
- Calculator
- Stirrer

---

3. Principle

Total Solids (TS) in milk is the **sum of fat and SNF**. It represents the **complete dry matter** of milk, excluding water. TS can be calculated using empirical values derived from lactometer and fat test readings:

TS = Fat % + SNF %

SNF is calculated using:

$$SNF = \frac{CLR}{4} + (0.25 \times Fat) + 0.44$$

Where:

- CLR = Corrected Lactometer Reading
- Fat % is determined using the **Gerber method**

---

4. Methodology

1. **Measure the lactometer reading (LR)** by inserting the lactometer into the milk sample.
2. **Note the temperature** of the milk using a thermometer.
3. Apply **temperature correction** to LR:
   - Add 0.2 for every °C above 27°C
   - Subtract 0.2 for every °C below 27°C

   $$CLR = LR \pm Temp\ correction$$

4. Determine **Fat %** by the **Gerber method** (or use an assumed value).
5. Calculate **SNF** using the formula:

$$SNF = \frac{CLR}{4} + (0.25 \times Fat) + 0.44$$

6. Calculate **Total Solids**:

   TS = fat + SNF

---

5. Observation

Parameter	**Value**
Lactometer Reading (LR)	30
Milk Temperature	28°C
Temperature Correction	+0.2
Corrected LR (CLR)	30.2
Fat % (from Gerber method)	4.5%

SNF (calculated)

$$= \frac{30.2}{4} + (0.25 \times 4.5) + 0.44$$

$$= 7.55 + 1.125 = 9.12\%$$

$$TS = 4.5 + 9.12 = 13.62\%$$

---

6. Conclusion

The **Total Solids content of the milk** sample is **13.62%**, which is within the **normal range for buffalo/cow milk (12–16%)**. A proper TS level indicates good **nutritional quality**, while significantly lower values may suggest **adulteration with water**.

Determining TS is crucial for **milk grading, pricing**, and **quality assurance** in the dairy industry.

6. Determination of Acidity and pH of Milk

---

1. Aim

To determine the **titratable acidity** and **pH** of a milk sample, which are important indicators of milk freshness and quality.

---

2. Materials and Methods

Materials Required:

- Fresh milk sample
- Standard N/10 NaOH solution
- Phenolphthalein indicator
- Burette, pipette, and conical flask
- pH meter or pH paper
- Measuring cylinder
- Beaker and stirrer

---

3. Principle

- **Titratable Acidity** measures the amount of **lactic acid** and other acid components in milk. It is determined by **titrating milk with NaOH** using phenolphthalein as an indicator.

- **pH** is a measure of the hydrogen ion concentration. Fresh milk has a **pH of about 6.6 to 6.8**. A drop in pH indicates increased acidity due to **microbial activity**.

---

4. Methodology

A. Titratable Acidity

1. Take **10 ml of milk** in a conical flask.
2. Add **2-3 drops of phenolphthalein indicator**.
3. Fill the burette with **N/10 NaOH solution**.
4. Titrate the milk solution until a **faint pink color** persists for 30 seconds.
5. Note the **volume of NaOH used**.
6. Calculate the **acidity** as % lactic acid using:

$$Acidity\ (\%Lactic\ Acid) = \frac{Vol\ of\ NaOH\ \times 0.009\ \times 100}{Volume\ of\ Milk\ Sample}$$

B. pH Determination

1. Calibrate the **pH meter** using standard buffer solutions.
2. Take **a small volume of milk** in a beaker.
3. Dip the **pH electrode** into the milk sample.
4. Record the **pH reading**. (Alternatively, use **pH paper** for approximate measurement.)

---

5. Observation

Parameter	Value
Volume of milk	10 ml
Volume of NaOH used	1.8 ml

$$Acidity\ (\%lactic\ acid) = \frac{1.8 \times 0.009 \times 100}{10} = 0.162\%$$

---

6. Conclusion

The **titratable acidity** of the milk sample was found to be **0.162%**, and the **pH was 6.7**, which indicates that the milk is **fresh and unspoiled**. Normal values for fresh milk:

- **Acidity**: 0.14% to 0.18%
- **pH**: 6.6 to 6.8

These tests are essential in **dairy quality control** to detect early signs of spoilage and ensure milk safety for processing or consumption.

7. Methylene Blue Reduction (MBR) Test of Milk

---

1. Aim

To perform the **Methylene Blue Reduction (MBR) test** for assessing the **microbial quality** of milk by estimating the number of viable bacteria present.

---

2. Materials and Methods

Materials Required:

- Fresh milk sample
- Methylene blue solution (0.005%)
- Test tubes (20 ml capacity)
- Pipettes
- Water bath or incubator (at 37°C)
- Test tube rack
- Stopwatch or timer

---

3. Principle

The MBR test is based on the principle that **methylene blue dye is reduced (decolorized)** by the metabolic activity of **microorganisms** present in milk.

- **Greater microbial load** → Faster reduction (discoloration) of dye

- **Longer time to decolorize** → Better milk quality

The time taken for the blue color to disappear indicates the **degree of bacterial contamination**.

---

4. Methodology

1. Take **10 ml of milk** in a clean test tube.
2. Add **1 ml of 0.005% methylene blue solution**.
3. Mix gently without forming foam.
4. Place the test tube in a **water bath at 37°C**.
5. Note the **time taken** for the blue color to **completely disappear**.
6. Record observations and compare with standard bacterial quality grades.

---

5. Observation

Time for Decolorization	Microbial Quality Grade
>5 hours	Excellent
3–5 hours	Good
1–2 hours	Fair
<30 minutes	Poor

Example:

Parameter	Value
Volume of milk	10 ml
Volume of methylene blue used	1 ml
Time taken for decolorization	3.5 hours
Quality Grade	Good

6. Conclusion

The milk sample took **3.5 hours** for the methylene blue dye to decolorize, indicating that the milk is of **Good microbial quality**.

The MBR test is a **quick, low-cost method** for assessing milk hygiene at collection centers and in dairy plants. It provides an **indirect estimate of bacterial load**, helping to ensure **safe processing and consumption**.

8. Determination of Phosphatase Activity in Milk

---

1. Aim

To determine the **phosphatase activity in milk**, which serves as an **indicator of proper pasteurization**.

---

2. Materials and Methods

Materials Required:

- Milk sample (raw and/or pasteurized)
- Buffer solution (disodium phosphate-citrate buffer, pH 9.8)
- Substrate: **p-nitrophenyl phosphate (PNPP)** or **phenolphthalein diphosphate**
- Water bath (maintained at 37°C or 40°C)
- Test tubes
- Colorimeter or spectrophotometer
- Stopper and pipettes
- Distilled water

---

3. Principle

Alkaline phosphatase is an enzyme naturally present in raw milk. It gets **inactivated at pasteurization temperatures (72°C for 15 seconds)**.

If **phosphatase activity is detected**, it means the milk is **either raw, improperly pasteurized, or contaminated**. The enzyme acts on a **specific substrate** (e.g., PNPP), producing a **colored compound** (e.g., p-nitrophenol), which can be measured spectrophotometrically.

---

4. Methodology

1. Take **5 ml of milk sample** in a clean test tube.
2. Add **1 ml of buffer solution (pH 9.8)**.
3. Add **1 ml of PNPP substrate**.
4. Mix well and incubate in a **water bath at 37°C for 30 minutes**.
5. After incubation, **stop the reaction** by placing the tube in ice-cold water or adding a stopping reagent (e.g., NaOH if using PNPP).
6. Measure the **color intensity** using a **colorimeter or spectrophotometer at 405 nm**.
7. Compare the results with a **control (boiled/pasteurized milk)**.

---

5. Observation

Sample Type	**Color Development**	**Absorbance (405 nm)**	**Phosphatase Activity**
Raw Milk	Yellow color	0.85	Active
Pasteurized Milk	No color change	0.05	Inactive

6. Conclusion

The **raw milk sample** showed **phosphatase activity**, confirming the presence of the enzyme and indicating that it is **unpasteurized**. The **pasteurized milk** showed **no activity**, confirming **proper pasteurization**.

The **phosphatase test** is a reliable method to **verify the effectiveness of pasteurization** and ensure **consumer safety** in the dairy industry.

9. Detection of Common Adulterants in Milk

---

1. Aim

To detect the presence of **common adulterants** in milk such as **water, starch, detergent, urea, and formalin**, using **simple chemical tests**.

---

2. Materials and Methods

Materials Required:

- Milk samples
- Test tubes and droppers
- Iodine solution (for starch test)
- Bromothymol blue or pH paper (for detergent test)
- Sodium hypochlorite and phenol red (for urea test)
- Sulphuric acid (for formalin test)
- Lactometer (for water dilution test)
- Distilled water
- Beakers, pipettes, safety gloves

---

3. Principle

Milk adulteration is done to increase volume or shelf life but poses **serious health hazards**. Each adulterant reacts with a **specific chemical reagent** to produce a **color change or characteristic reaction**, indicating its presence.

---

4. Methodology

A. Detection of Water (Dilution)

- Use a **lactometer** to check the **specific gravity** of milk.
- Normal range: **1.026–1.032**
- **Low reading** indicates **added water**.

B. Detection of Starch

- Take 3 ml of milk in a test tube.
- Add **2–3 drops of iodine solution**.
- **Blue color** indicates **presence of starch**.

C. Detection of Detergent

- Take 5 ml of milk in a test tube.
- Shake well and add **5 ml of distilled water**.
- Formation of **dense foam** indicates **detergent**.
- pH test: Add **bromothymol blue**; **blue color** shows alkaline detergent.

D. Detection of Urea

- Add **0.2 ml sodium hypochlorite** and **0.1 ml phenol red** to 5 ml of milk.

- **Pink color** within 10 minutes confirms **urea**.

E. Detection of Formalin

- Take 5 ml of milk in a test tube.
- Gently add **5 ml of concentrated sulphuric acid** from the side wall.
- Formation of **violet or blue ring** at the junction confirms **formalin**.

---

5. Observation

Adulterant	Test Performed	Result	Inference
Water	Lactometer reading	1.022	Water added
Starch	Iodine test	Blue color	Starch present
Detergent	Foam and pH test	Persistent foam	Detergent present
Urea	Hypochlorite + Phenol red test	Pink color	Urea present
Formalin	Sulphuric acid ring test	Violet ring	Formalin present

---

6. Conclusion

The tests confirmed the presence of **multiple adulterants** in the milk sample including **water, starch, detergent, urea, and formalin**.

These simple and quick tests are essential for **routine quality checks** at **milk collection centers and households** to ensure **consumer safety** and **public health**.

10. Format for Dairy Farm Visit Report

---

1. Title Page

- Title: *Report on Visit to [Name of Dairy Farm]*
- Name of Student
- Roll Number / ID
- Institution Name
- Date of Visit
- Submitted to (Instructor/Department)

---

2. Acknowledgement

- Brief note thanking the institution, faculty, and dairy farm staff for arranging and facilitating the visit.

---

3. Introduction

- Purpose of the visit
- Objectives of the study
- Importance of dairy farming in rural economy and food industry

---

4. General Information about the Dairy Farm

- Name and location of the dairy farm
- Type of dairy farm: Small-scale/Commercial/Cooperative
- Ownership: Private, Government, SHG-run, etc.
- Area covered and infrastructure details

---

5. Livestock and Breeds

- Types of animals maintained (cows, buffaloes, etc.)
- Breeds (e.g., Sahiwal, Jersey, Holstein Friesian)
- Total number of animals
- Breeding practices followed

---

6. Feeding and Nutrition

- Types of fodder and feed used
- Feed storage and rationing system
- Supplementation and mineral mix usage

---

7. Milking Practices

- Milking method (manual or machine)
- Frequency of milking
- Hygiene and clean milk production practices
- Use of antiseptics or pre/post-milking teat dips

---

8. Animal Health and Veterinary Care

- Vaccination and deworming schedules
- Disease management practices
- Availability of veterinary services
- Record keeping

---

9. Milk Storage and Transportation

- Milk collection and cooling methods
- Storage tanks and chilling facilities
- Transportation to collection canters or markets

---

10. Waste Management

- Handling of dung and urine
- Use of biogas plants or compost pits
- Environmental management practices

---

11. Observations and Learnings

- Key observations made during the visit
- Innovative or sustainable practices
- Gaps or challenges observed
- Learnings relevant to academic and practical understanding

---

12. Conclusion

- Summary of the visit
- Relevance to coursework or future entrepreneurship
- Suggestions for improvements or innovations

---

13. Photographs (if permitted)

- Images of livestock, infrastructure, feed storage, milking area, etc.

---

14. Annexure (Optional)

- Farm layout diagram
- Sample data sheets or records maintained by the farm
- Interview notes (if any)

Index

E

F

G

M

N

O

P

R

S

T

www.ingramcontent.com/pod-product-compliance
Ingram Content Group UK Ltd.
Pitfield, Milton Keynes, MK11 3LW, UK
UKHW021649190726
13853UKWH00001B/151

9 798899 619922